NORWAY

GROLIER

A ....ishing

Published for Grolier,
an imprint of Scholastic Library Publishing
Old Sherman Turnpike, Danbury, Connecticut 06816
by Times Editions,
an imprint of Times Media Pte Ltd

Set ISBN: 0-7172-5788-6
Volume ISBN: 0-7172-5798-3

Library of Congress Cataloging-in-Publication Data
Norway.
p. cm.—(Fiesta!)
Summary: Discusses the festivals and holidays of Norway and how the songs, food,
and traditions associated with these celebrations reflect the culture of the people.
1. Festivals—Norway—Juvenile literature. 2. Norway—Social life and customs—Juvenile literature.
[1. Festivals—Norway. 2. Holidays—Norway. 3. Norway—Social life and customs.]
I. Grolier (Firm). II. Fiesta! (Danbury, Conn.)
GT4860.A2N67   2004
394.26481—dc21   2003044846

For this volume
Author: Christoph Brunski
Editor: Balvinder Sandhu
Designer: Benson Tan
Production: Nor Sidah Haron
Crafts and Recipes produced by Stephen Russell

Printed in Malaysia

Adult supervision advised for all crafts and recipes,
particularly those involving sharp instruments and heat.

CONTENTS

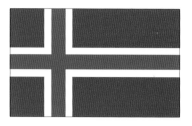

NORWAY:

Norway is part of Scandinavia, an area of land in Northern Europe that also includes Sweden and Denmark. Norway is bordered by Sweden to the east and Denmark to the south. Most of Norway stretches along the Atlantic Ocean.

NORWEGIAN SEA

Trondheim

OSLO

Baerum

▲ **Fjords** are the most distinctive part of Norway's geography. They are areas where deep mountain cliffs are met by the ocean, forming long passages of water along the coast. The fjords are a popular spot for tourists to visit.

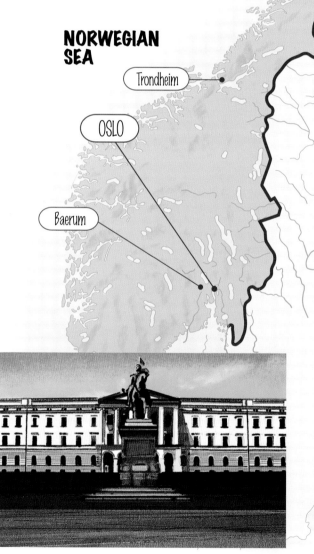

▶ Oslo is the capital city of Norway. It was founded in 1050 and is the location of the **Royal Palace**. It is a very lively city with a lot of cultural activities. About 500,000 people live in Oslo.

Tromsø

Arctic Circle

SWEDEN

FINLAND

▲ In the very northern part of Norway there is a group of people called the **Sami**. The Sami are reindeer herders and fishermen, and speak their own language, which is different from the rest of the country.

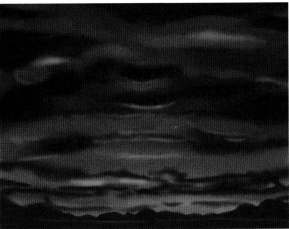

▶ Part of Norway is above the Arctic Circle. This means that the year is dark all winter long and light all summer long. It has given Norway the name **"Land of the Midnight Sun."**

RELIGIONS

Norway is mainly a Christian country. Olav I, Olav Tryggvason, brought
Christianity from England to Norway around the year 995 A.D. It was Olav II,
Olav Haraldsson, who continued the Christianization of the country.

AT FIRST, the Norwegians practiced Christianity in the same way as people from other European countries. However, that changed dramatically after a few hundred years.

Martin Luther, who was German, had a very big influence on Christianity in Norway. Luther believed that scripture was the only religious authority, and that one's deeds alone did not lead to salvation. This was often expressed by the Latin phrase *sola gratia per fidem*, which means "of grace alone." This idea, called the Reformation, came to Norway in 1536. Norway's schools taught lessons that were mainly connected to religion.

The importance of Pietism is another thing that makes Norway's Christianity different from other countries. Pietism means that there is a more personal connection with God. Even though a person might go to church services and

Every church in Norway has hymn books, which are used by the congregation during a service.

pray, that person has to do more to be pious. He or she has to personally surrender to God. This idea plays more of a role in the Church of Norway than it does in Roman Catholic countries.

In modern times there are still many people who are active in the Church of Norway. Norway's king has power over the church, and many of the decisions

6

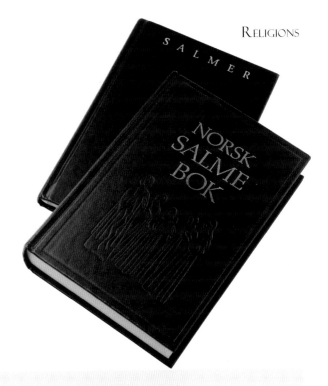

that royalty has made for the church over the years reflect modern ideas. For example, women now hold many of the highest positions in the Church of Norway.

Although the Constitution says that everyone has the right to practice the religion of their choice, the Evangelical-Lutheran religion of the Church of Norway is the official state religion. However, the world's major religions are all represented in Norway, where diversity is welcomed.

GREETINGS FROM **NORWAY!**

Norway is a country with a very interesting language. The language is called Norwegian and is similar to English in many ways. However, there are two official types of Norwegian. They are called *Bokmål* and *Nynorsk*. Newspapers and books are written in each of these languages. These two types of Norwegian have slight variations in spelling; but when Norwegians talk, everyone understands each other, no matter which kind of Norwegian they use.

How do you say...

Hello
Hei!

Please
Vennligst

How are you?
Hvordan står det til?

Goodbye!
Ha det!

Thank you
Takk!

LUCIA DAY

Although it's not celebrated as grandly as in Sweden, Norwegians do recognize Lucia Day. It is the longest night of the year, and from then till Christmas Day spirits, gnomes, and trolls roam the earth.

Lucia Day falls on December 13, and children in Norway play a big part in the celebration. In every town nearly every church or school has its own Lucia procession.

In the procession one girl plays the part of Lucia. She wears a white gown and a headpiece with several lighted candles. Lucia is followed by other girls who are also dressed in white. They sing a song that tells the story of St. Lucia. The procession visits hospitals and nursing homes to serve coffee and *Lussekattor* buns to the elderly residents.

Lussekattor are special buns made on Lucia Day. They are baked with saffron and then tied into a knotted shape. They are a delicious treat that children love.

Lucia Day is a saint's day. Many early Christians in Scandinavia had a fondness for St. Lucia, whose name means "light."

Many people believe that St. Lucia took food

Norwegians believe that creatures such as trolls roam the earth in the time between Lucia Day and Christmas. One ancient Norwegian tale tells of how a troll saved the life of a princess.

and water to the early Christians when they were under persecution.

To light her way through the night, she wore a crown adorned with candles. In ancient times the children would write the word *Lussi* on

On Lucia Day Norwegians eat Lussekattor, *which are knotted buns baked with saffron.*

their doors to pay tribute to St. Lucia. This was a way of promising that the long and cold winter would soon be replaced by the brightness of sun and the spring.

Lucia Day is often seen as the beginning of the Christmas season. The lighting of the candles and the singing of the Lucia song make people think of Christmas carols, and the Lucia procession helps get people ready for a festive season that lasts all the way to the new year.

Although trolls are supposed to be very fierce, the two-headed troll is a friendly one and shouldn't be feared.

MAKE A LUCIA CROWN

YOU WILL NEED
Light craft wire
Fine twigs
Aluminum foil
Small birthday candles

You can make your own Lucia Crown, just like the one used in the processions held in Norway.

1 Take the twigs, and braid them together in a circular pattern. Use pieces of wire to help them stay attached. Make several layers of the circle so that the crown is sturdy, like a small wreath.

2 Wrap a small, thin strip of foil about one inch wide around the base of the candles until you have created a thicker base for each candle. It will hold the candle in place in the crown.

3 Insert the candles into the crown opposite each other. Push the candles into the twigs of the crown so they are stable.

CHRISTMAS

The essence of Norwegian festivals, Christmas is a time for family, fun, and food! It also involves special traditions, church services, and chopping down Christmas trees!

This motherly figure is Julenisse's wife, another popular character during Christmas for Norwegians.

For the Norwegians *Jul*, or Christmas, is a favorite time of year. It is perhaps the time of year that is surrounded with the most tradition and festivity.

All throughout the season leading up to Christmas there are town fairs and concerts. They most often feature many seasonal treats, such as ginger cookies and candy.

Norwegians often go into the forest to choose their own Christmas tree. During the afternoon of Christmas Eve church bells ring for a long time to announce the official start

Julenisse is the Norwegian Santa Claus. On Christmas Eve children leave a bowl of porridge out for him, to thank him for watching over them during the year.

of the Christmas holiday. The Christmas tree is then decorated and lighted in the house later that evening.

Children who live in the countryside have a special tradition they carry out on Christmas Eve. Norwegians have long thought that farms and country houses were protected by a *nisse*, or gnome. The *nisse* of recent

MAKE A "JULEKURV" (CHRISTMAS BASKET)

YOU WILL NEED
Colored paper
Scissors
Glue or tape

1 On the noncolored side of the origami paper trace the shape of a circular object, such as a teacup or a glass. Repeat this step on a sheet of paper of a different color or pattern.

2 Cut out the circles, and fold each circle in half.

3 Open one circle slightly, and insert the other so that the flat sides of each shape form right angles.

4 Glue the pieces together in this arrangement. Make sure that the glue does not run into the center of the basket so it can still be opened slightly..

5 Cut out one longer section to use as a "handle" for the basket.

6 When the glue has dried, open the basket slightly. You may have to crease the paper to give it shape.

7 Hang on your Christmas Tree!

Norwegians often wear sweaters and headbands during the festive season. These clothing are usually in the Christmas colors of red or green.

having kept watch over the farm, and ensuring that he will stay on the farm to continue bringing wealth and good health to the people living there.

A church service is held early on Christmas morning. After the service families return home to begin an early dinner. The Christmas meal is a large feast and includes many traditional foods.

One of these foods is *lutefisk*, which is a type of codfish that is soft and jellylike. Children often do not like the taste of *lutefisk* very much, but

Norwegians use a special spoon like the one below to sprinkle sugar over the Christmas porridge. Porridge is a popular dish during the festive season, and some families serve it in specially designed bowls, such as the one on the right.

years has become much like the St. Nicholas of other countries.

Children carry a bowl of porridge out to the barn for the gnome to eat. It is to thank him for

NORWEGIAN CHRISTMAS PORRIDGE

Christmas porridge is a traditional favorite among Norwegians during the festive season.

SERVES 4

1 quart milk
1 cup rice (special rice for porridge)
A pinch of salt
A lump of butter
A sprinkling of sugar and cinammon

1 Bring the milk to a boil.

2 Add the rice to the milk, and let it simmer for 45 minutes or until it gets thick. Be careful, and stir it from time to time to avoid burning.

3 Add a pinch of salt, and serve the porridge while it's hot.

4 On your plate put a small lump of butter in the middle of your portion, and drizzle sugar and cinammon on top.

it is an important dish that is served at holiday meals.

The main dish is pork, which can be prepared following different recipes. There are also many other rich and delicious items to eat, including puddings and cakes.

What the majority of Norwegian children love most about Christmas is the special celebration surrounding the Christmas tree. The whole family joins hands and forms a large ring around the tree, then dances around it while they sing songs and laugh.

Knitting sweaters for the extremely cold Christmas season is a popular hobby among older women in Norway.

CONSTITUTION DAY

This is the day of Norwegian independence and pride, when Norwegians take part in street parades, wearing their national costume, and waving their flags.

Constitution Day, on May 17, is an important day for Norway, which used to be ruled by countries such as Sweden and Denmark.

It was on this date in 1814 that the Norwegian constitution was written, and the country became self-governing. Norway's capital, Oslo, used to be known as Christiania, to honor a Danish king. Once the Norwegians had their own sovereignty, the name of the city was changed back to Oslo.

Constitution Day is celebrated by both young and old in the country. Children take part in colorful parades and sing national songs such as *Ja, vi elsker dette landet* (Yes, we love our country).

The streets in the city are lined with flags and banners. Wreaths are also laid on monuments to honor famous Norwegians.

Parades are held all over the country, with the biggest taking place in Oslo. This parade ends in front of the palace, where the royal family greets the crowd.

Feeling patriotic pride on May 17 also goes along with feeling happy and comfortable, since this special celebration takes place just as the weather is getting warmer again.

On Constitution Day many people wear a traditional Norwegian dress known as a *bunad*. It is a colorful costume with patterns that represent the different parts of the country each group comes from.

In order to achieve independence, Norwegians worked very hard. A lot of manual work was done with the help of horse-drawn carriages.

Children enjoy eating the many tarts and cookies that are baked specially for the ocassion.

Norwegian children commemorate Constitution Day by taking part in parades and singing national songs.

When children march in the Constitution Day parades, they wear *bunads* to show that they are proud of the town or region in which they live. However, they also carry the Norwegian flag to show that they are proud overall to be Norwegian.

JA, VI ELSKER DETTE LANDET

Ja vi elsker dette landet som det stiger frem

furet vaerbitt over vannet med de tusen hjem

elsker elsker det og tenker på vår far og mor

og den saganatt som senker drømme på vår jord

Yes, we love with fond devotion
This our land that looms
Rugged, storm-scarred o'er the ocean
With her thousand homes
Love her, in our love recalling
Those who gave us birth
And old tales which night in falling
Brings as dreams to earth

EASTER

A festival that also means ringing in the springtime, Easter is a time for families to get together and commemorate the occasion with both religious and traditional celebrations.

The Norwegian word for Easter is Påske. Easter in Norway is a period when everyone has some free time – children have a short break from school, and adults take some time away from work.

Many people all over Norway look forward to Easter with excitement. Most families spend this time together celebrating the holiday and practicing several Easter traditions.

On Easter Day many Norwegians wake up early to attend a religious Mass.

The service is often held outdoors in order to see the sun rise. This is a way for Christians to recognize the resurrection of Christ.

Flowers such as tulips and daffodils often bloom in Norway around Easter. Children go out to gather big bouquets of flowers.

Children in Norway play games with painted eggs on Easter. Contests such as egg rolling are held. In this game they see who can push an egg the farthest either by blowing

on it or pushing it with their nose.

Another game that the children play is called egg tapping. In this game they tap the eggs together to see whose egg can survive uncracked the longest.

Tulips bloom in Norway around Easter, and children gather bouquets of them.

An ancient tradition in Norway is to leave a special brew outside the house the Thursday before Easter. This is because people living in remote areas used to believe in witches, and the brew was thought to keep them away during Easter.

Another tradition that is still practiced in Norway today has to do with detective and mystery stories. No one is quite sure why, but

Easter is also the time of year when Norwegians read detective novels and watch detective shows on TV. This funny tradition is known as Easter Crime!

In the past Norwegians used a dish like this to serve bread.

NORWEGIAN EASTER MARZIPAN

YOU WILL NEED
1 lb almonds, blanched and skins removed
1 lb powdered sugar
1 egg white

1 Grind the almonds. Add sugar, and mix well.

2 Add the egg white, and mix. Note: A small quantity of rose water can be used instead of egg white.

3 Store in the refrigerator, and add food coloring if desired.

4 When rolling out marzipan, use powdered sugar to keep it from sticking.

ST. OLAV'S DAY SALMON

In this legend village fishermen tell how they predict the weather with the salmon that they catch on St. Olav's Day, which falls on July 29.

A BIG GROUP of fishermen were once talking about the size of the salmon that they had caught at various times of the year. One fisherman said that the salmon he had caught on St. Olav's Day were all long and thin, and not very good to eat.

Another fisherman said that the same thing happened to him. The salmon he caught on the last St. Olav's Day were long and not very fat, and the whole year that followed was full of bad weather with lots of rain.

Several of the other fishermen told the same tale and agreed that the weather had been bad the whole season after St. Olav's Day.

From that day onward all the fishermen began to compare the fish they caught whenever they went fishing on St. Olav's Day, and they realized that there was a familiar pattern to the size of the fish and the weather that came that year.

Every year when the salmon were long and thin, the year that followed was rainy and windy. If the salmon bled a lot when they were loaded onto the boat, there was always a lot of thunder. However, when the salmon were fat and strong, the following year would be a bountiful year with sunny and beautiful weather. The fishermen then realized that there was a message in the size of the salmon that they caught on St. Olav's Day.

To this day, when the salmon come into shore on this holiday, the fishermen pay careful attention to their size, since they now believe that they will be able to forecast the weather just by looking at the size of the St. Olav's Day salmon!

MIDSUMMER

An ancient rite celebrating the summer months, Midsummer traditions include wearing a Midsummer crown, putting on "play" weddings, and dancing around the Midsummer pole.

Children pick bunches of wildflowers for Midsummer, weave them into a crown, and wear them.

Sankhansaften, also called Midsummer's Eve, is celebrated on June 23. This festival was originally named for John the Baptist, but it is also a holiday that is intimately connected with ancient beliefs about the summer solstice. People believed that this longest day was a time of great magic, and many rituals centered on this day.

It was believed that Midsummer wildflowers possessed a miraculous healing power, and people picked them on this special night in the hope of health and prosperity. Since magic was in the air, the people built bonfires to keep witches and evil spirits away.

Children today still gather huge bunches of wildflowers, and they weave them into a type of crown that they wear while they dance on Midsummer's Eve.

Some Norwegians still practice an ancient tradition that involves putting on a "pretend" wedding between

Building a bonfire for Midsummer is an ancient tradition that still takes place today. In the past it was done to drive away evil spirits.

adults and children. This wedding represents the continuation of life and hope for the happiness of the children.

Today the people of Norway still continue the tradition of building great bonfires and dancing into the late hours of sunlight.

Even more important are the Midsummer poles. They are big tree trunks that are decorated and set upright. They symbolize fertility and abundance, and during the Midsummer festivities people dance and sing around them.

A popular Midsummer tradition is a "wedding" that takes place between children and adults.

VI SKAL IKKJE SOVA BORT SUMARNATTA

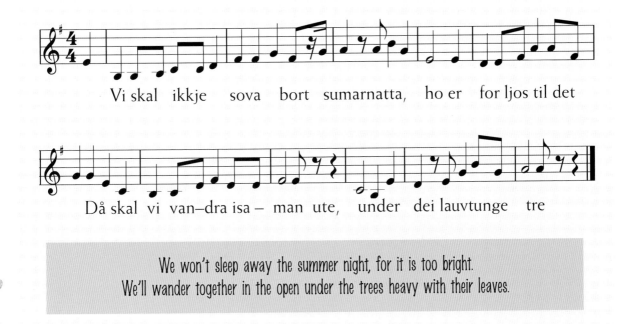

Vi skal ikkje sova bort sumarnatta, ho er for ljos til det

Då skal vi van–dra isa – man ute, under dei lauvtunge tre

We won't sleep away the summer night, for it is too bright.
We'll wander together in the open under the trees heavy with their leaves.

THE SWANS AND THE NORTHERN LIGHTS

This legend, from the Sami people, tells of a mystical source of the northern lights, and how it contains an important lesson about living in the north of Norway.

A SAMI BOY, looking up with wonder at the northern lights (aurora borealis) asked his father where they came from. His father told him that once, in the cold and frozen fields of the north, a flock of swans was flying. The swans, like most groups of birds, had their regular places to fly in and had their regular spots to land and stay the night in safety.

But one evening a particular flock of swans kept on flying past the areas they knew well. The sun was setting, and the warmth of the day was beginning to disappear. But the swans did not land. They went farther and farther north, until it was extremely cold and dark. The swans did not recognize anything any longer. There was little moonlight for them to see where they were.

Finally, they had flown so far that they could fly no more. They were at the top of the world. The swans had to land and rest, for they had been in the air for an entire day. They were on the ground for a short time when they realized that they did not belong in this place; it was too cold and too dangerous for them, and too far from their home.

Instead of waiting any longer, they decided it would be best to return home. But when they tried to take off again, they found that their wings had become stuck to the ice where they had landed. The freezing cold held them fast to the ground. They struggled to get free from the ice; and even though they could not get away, their wings sent huge sprays of snow and ice into the air. These fine and frozen particles flew through the air in a southerly direction, flashing through the sky in brilliant and shimmering colors.

The people who saw these streaks in the sky called them the aurora borealis. They took them to mean that they should

respect the power of the northern cold and not stray too far into it without thinking.

"Whoever sees the northern lights," said the boy's father, "should remember the lesson that those swans have taught us – that the mysterious powers of the north are to be admired and obeyed. One should not be so foolish, whether animal or human, to think that these powers can be beaten."

THE NORTHERN LIGHTS FESTIVAL

A celebration of the aurora borealis, this festival in the north of Norway includes music and dancing, and highlights the culture of the Sami.

The Northern Lights Festival is a unique event that captures the spirit of the north. It is one of Norway's newer festivals and is held every January in Tromsø, one of the cities in the northern part of the country.

Life in this area can be hard because of the harsh climate – there is extreme cold, and most of the year is wintry and dark. But northern Norway is blessed with one of nature's most spectacular phenomena – the aurora

The cold weather in northern Norway means that its residents are wrapped up in winter clothes for the most part of the year. Many Norwegians also wear shoes made from reindeer skin, since the boots keep their feet warm in freezing temperatures.

Children in the north of Norway wrap themselves up to keep warm and then go out to play.

borealis which is also called the northern lights.

Jazz, folk music, and dancing go on till late in the night throughout the festival, when people come together to keep their spirits high during the cold months. At any time one can look up into the sky and see the wonderful shapes of the northern lights putting on their own performance for everyone to behold.

This festival also highlights the culture of the Sami, a people who live in the north and other parts of Scandinavia. The Sami, who live by herding reindeer, are especially connected to the beauty of the Northern Lights, which dance across the sky in brilliant waves of shimmering color.

Children who come from larger cities in Norway might never have met a Sami before. At this festival children learn from the Samis how they herd their reindeer, and how they have a special way of singing known as *Joik.*

It is extremely cold in Tromsø most of the year, and skiing is one of the activities that can be enjoyed there.

While the Norwegians meet people from different parts of their country at this festival, the event also attracts others from all around the world who come to see the miracle of the aurora borealis, and enjoy the music.

BARNAS CHILDREN'S FESTIVAL

The Barnas Festival is held to celebrate children, the future of Norway, and they have loads of fun while learning about the cultures of Norway and the world.

Fun is a key element of the Barnas Festival, as enjoyable activities are organized especially for children to have a good time.

Although it is a relatively new festival, the Barnas Festival has grown in popularity and has recently attracted 40,000 visitors.

Another new festival enjoyed by Norwegians is the Barnas Festival. This festival held in the town of Bærum has many special events for children and is so large that they come from all over the country to take part in the festivities and activities.

Over the years this festival has become more popular and has had more to offer the children who come to visit. In recent years as many as 40,000 visitors have come to this unique celebration.

Barnas Festival was created for one reason alone – the celebration of children in Norway. Hundreds of entertainers and teachers participate in the festival. The goal of this unique holiday is for children to have fun and to learn new things. The Barnas Festival aims to make children aware of the culture of Norway and countries around the world.

One feature of the festival is dance instruction for types of dances that come from all over the globe. Some of the many other activities include a music workshops, Lego-building contest, painting classes, trampoline centers, sporting events, and many other enjoyable things.

Children at the Barnas Festival are also taught about Norway's unique natural environment and some of the animal species living in it.

Children are very important to the future of any country, and the leaders of the Barnas Festival recognize that Norway will be a better country tomorrow than it is today if children are given the best chances to learn and develop their interests and talents.

During the Barnas Festival children also get to learn about the cultures of Norway and other countries.

Norwegians place great importance on children, since they are the future of the country.

29

ALL SAINTS DAY

Originally held on two consecutive days, All Saints Day and All Souls Day are now combined as one. It's a solemn memorial, but has lately started to adopt traditions from the American Halloween celebrations.

On November 1 *Allehelgens Dag*, or All Saints Day, is celebrated by Norwegians. In the past on the next day they remembered those who had passed away. For this reason these days were called All Saints Day and All Souls Day.

Now both ceremonies are combined into one. On this day people put candles and wreaths on gravestones to remember loved ones who have died. The sight of candles in the cemeteries under a darkened sky is solemn, but beautiful and moving.

The celebration at the end of October and the beginning of November has its origin in Celtic traditions. The first of November is considered to be the end of the year. These are also the roots of Halloween, which is celebrated in America and in other countries.

In recent years many children in Norway have started to adopt American

On All Saints Day lighted candles are put on gravestones in remembrance of those who have passed away.

Halloween traditions. They dress up in costumes and go from house to house for sweets. Since the weather begins to get quite dark and cold at this time of year, this is a way to have a little extra enjoyment before the harsh winter.

Norwegian children have started to adopt American Halloween traditions for All Saints Day.

WORDS TO KNOW

Artifacts: A handmade object, such as a tool, or the remains of one, such as a shard of pottery, belonging to an earlier time or cultural stage.

Aurora borealis: Bright and colorful lights that are formed in the sky at night when the air molecules react with the particles carried by the solar wind.

Bountiful: Generous in bestowing gifts or favors.

Celtic: Of or pertaining to the Celts, that is, Irish, Scottish, or Welsh.

Commemorate: To honor the memory of someone or an event by a special ceremony.

Constitution: A set of rules by which a nation is governed.

Distinctive: Having a special quality or style that makes it attractive.

Gnome: A dwarflike being that lives in the center of the Earth.

Mystical: Having to do with mysterious forces that people cannot understand.

Persecution: To be subjected to harrassment or cruel treatment because of religion, race, or beliefs.

Procession: A large group of people moving in an orderly fashion, usually in a line.

Salvation: Deliverance from the power and penalty of sin; redemption.

Scripture: The sacred writings of the Old or New Testament of the Bible.

Solstice: One of the two times a year when the sun is at its greatest distance from the equator.

Troll: Any of a race of supernatural beings, usually hostile to humans, who live underground, or in caves.

Vikings: People of Scandinavia who lived between the 8th and 11th centuries; they engaged in trade and often attacked and robbed other countries in the area.

ACKNOWLEDGMENTS

WITH THANKS TO:
Monica Kragholm of The Norwegian Seamen's Mission, Marianne Flatla Grandum of the Norwegian Business Association, Kristin Sim, Marguerita Tan, and Chiang Yuenling.

PHOTOGRAPHS BY:
Haga Library, Japan (cover, p. 22 bottom left). Yu Hui Ying (All other images).

ILLUSTRATIONS BY:
Enrico Sallustio (p. 1), Ang Lee Ming (p. 4 left), Amy Ong (p. 4 right, p. 5 both, p. 7), Ong Lay Keng (pp. 18-19), Lee Kowling (p. 25)

SET CONTENTS